TOTALLY KOREAN

*Traditional Korean Dishes
You Can Make at Home
(2022 Guide for Beginners)*

Eugene Kim

Table of content

Introduction

There are numerous cuisines around the world, each telling its own story about the region's history and culture. So often, a single bite of authentic regional cuisine contains the stories and secrets of generations. Each ingredient and flavor used to create the dish is a tribute to the area's natural resources. There are differences between the cuisines of neighboring countries or cultures, which can be minor or significant. All of these characteristics can be found in Korean cuisine. Korean cuisine is often viewed as a subtle offshoot of the other styles of the region; however, a closer look reveals that Korean cuisine truly stands alone in the uniqueness and complexity of flavors. Many of the ingredients used in various Asian cuisines are the same; however, it is in the ingredients used to flavor the foods that Korea excels, providing the world with beautiful, rich, and perfectly spiced examples of how to make the most of native ingredients.

The depth of flavor in Korean food is the most noticeable feature. Koreans have mastered the use of pungent ingredients, allowing them to delicately layer each flavor to create dishes that are memorable and cherished around the world. Consider spicy red peppers mashed into a pungent paste, delicate spring onions, sweet and spicy ginger, and delectable ferments. One would think that combining all of these flavors in a single dish would be overwhelming, but the opposite is true. You can have all of these in a single dish in Korean cuisine, and instead of being overwhelmed, you will be intrigued and culinary intoxicated.

As you begin or continue your exploration of Korean cuisine, there are a few ingredients that will become pantry staples. Some of these ingredients are only available in well-stocked Korean markets. As a result, the recipes include more commonly found substitutes. This list will help you stock your home pantry to make every dish in this book if you have access to a good Korean market or a grocery store with a well-stocked international section.

Gochugaru (Korean chile powder/flakes): This powder is made from ground Korean red chiles and comes in two textures: fine and coarse. In recipes that call for cayenne powder or crushed red pepper flakes, use this instead.

Korean chile paste (Gochujang): Although spicy, this paste has a slightly sweet flavor that makes it irresistible. Chile paste can be found in a variety of dishes, including soups, salads, and marinades. The ingredients are listed as spicy chile paste in this book. While you can substitute another type of chile paste, the results will be different. If you're using a less sweet paste, make sure to balance the heat with a little sugar, honey, or corn syrup to give it a more authentic Korean flavor.

Fermented soybean paste (Doenjang): This paste, similar to miso, is ideal for soups and sauces. When possible, pick this over any other option.

Sticky rice cakes: These can be made from scratch or bought ready-made. They are sticky cakes made from sweet rice powder, often in the shape of small logs. You can get them fresh or dried. If you're using dried beans, soak them in water to soften them before using them.

Kimchi is a delicious fermented cabbage and sometimes another vegetable condiment. Kimchi can be purchased or made at home. Kimchi varies in flavor intensity and spiciness, so you may want to experiment with different ferments to find the kimchi you like best.

Korean soy sauce (Ganjang): Korean soy sauce is lighter in color and flavor than traditional soy sauce. Soups and delicate, broth-like sauces benefit the most from the use of Korean soy sauce. This can be used in recipes that call for soy sauce.

Rice wine (Mirim): A mildly sweet cooking wine ideal for marinating meats and dressing vegetables.

Sesame oil: A lightly nutty oil that can be used in cooking or as a salad dressing. It has a pleasant sesame flavor. Use with caution because a little can go a long way in terms of flavor.

Short grain white rice: This type of rice has a stickier texture when cooked than long grain or other types of rice. It's great for storing sauces and using them in rolls and desserts.

Glass noodles, also known as sweet potato noodles, are a clear type of noodle made from starch, most commonly sweet potato starch. When properly cooked, they are somewhat firm with a nice bite.

Scallions, garlic, ginger, onion, carrot, cabbage, Korean radish, and Korean pear are all required ingredients.

You'll discover that you can make an incredible variety of Korean dishes with just a few ingredients. The recipes in this book were designed to provide you with a foundation of dishes to introduce you to the world of Korean cuisine and inspire you to learn and experiment with cultural cooking more.

Gimbap (Seaweed Rolls) (Seaweed Rolls)

10 minutes to prepare

Preparation Time: 25 minutes

8 people

Ingredients: 1 pound lean steak, thinly sliced

14 cup sesame oil, crushed red pepper flakes, divided teaspoons

1 teaspoon soy sauce

14 cups sliced scallions 14 tablespoons brown sugar 1 teaspoon sea salt

1 teaspoon ground black pepper

8 cups cooked short-grain white rice

2 tbsp. rice vinegar

10 sheets lightly toasted seaweed paper 12 cups spicy kimchi, prepared

12 cups carrots, sliced into thin matchsticks

2 tablespoons sesame oil, red pepper flakes, soy sauce, brown sugar, scallions, salt, and black pepper in a medium-sized glass bowl Mix in the steak slices thoroughly. Allow marinating for 15 minutes.

Drizzle the rice vinegar and remaining sesame oil over the rice and toss to combine. Place aside.

In a skillet over medium heat, combine the steak and marinade. Cook for 5-7 minutes, or until the meat is cooked to your liking. Set aside after removing from the heat.

On a bamboo rolling mat, place a sheet of seaweed paper.

Spread 12 to 34 cups of rice on 34 pieces of seaweed paper, leaving 1-2 inches uncovered at the farthest end away from you.

Arrange a row of steak strips across the center of the seaweed paper, followed by kimchi and carrots.

Use the bamboo mat to help you tightly roll the seaweed with both hands. Roll first, then tuck tightly before pulling or pushing out the mat with your hand and rolling again. Repeat this pattern until the entire sheet is tightly rolled. Remove the mat and repeat with the remaining rolls.

Place the finished rolls on a cutting board and cut them into 1-inch thick pieces.

Serve right away.

Pancakes with shrimp and scallions

15 minutes to prepare

Preparation Time: 10 minutes

4-6 people

1 12 cups all-purpose flour 14 teaspoon baking powder

12 teaspoons black pepper 12 teaspoons salt

1 tablespoon red pepper flakes, crushed

14 cups ice-cold water

1 lightly beaten egg

12 pounds cleaned and chopped shrimp

4 cup scallions, cut into large chunks

1 cup diced red bell pepper

3 tbsp of soy sauce

1 tablespoon vinegar (rice)

1 tbsp sesame oil

1 tsp. lime juice

1 teaspoon grated fresh ginger

1 teaspoon toasted sesame seeds Vegetable oil for cooking

In a mixing bowl, whisk together the flour, baking powder, salt, pepper, and crushed red pepper flakes.

Whisk the flour with the water and egg until a thin batter forms. The batter should have the consistency of a thin pancake batter. If it is too thick, add a little more cold water until the desired consistency is reached.

Combine the shrimp, scallions, and red bell pepper in a mixing bowl. Set aside after thorough coating.

Combine the soy sauce, rice vinegar, sesame oil, lime juice, ginger, and sesame seeds in a mixing bowl. Combine thoroughly. Set aside for dipping purposes.

In a skillet, heat a thin layer of vegetable oil over medium heat.

Spoon the pancake batter into the pan with a ladle, making pancakes about 4 inches in diameter.

Cook for 2-3 minutes, or until the edges start to brown, before flipping and cooking for 3 minutes more.

Remove from the heat and serve with the dipping sauce while still warm.

Korean Sticky Chicken Wings

10 minutes to prepare

Preparation Time: 10 minutes

6 people

1 tablespoon sesame oil 2 pounds assorted chicken wings and drummettes, skin removed

1 tablespoon vinegar (rice)

4 garlic cloves, crushed and minced, divided

1 finely diced chile pepper

1 teaspoon grated fresh ginger

1 tablespoon cornstarch

1 teaspoon black pepper 1 teaspoon salt

14 tbsp soy sauce

14 cups garlic and chile paste 2 tbsp. ketchup, 2 tbsp. honey, 2 tbsp. apricot preserves

12 cups chopped red bell pepper 12 cups chopped scallions three tbsp rice wine

Fryable vegetable oil

Mix together the sesame oil, rice vinegar, half of the crushed garlic, chile pepper, and freshly grated ginger. Combine thoroughly.

Drizzle the mixture over the chicken wings in a bowl. Set aside after tossing to coat.

Combine the cornstarch, salt, and black pepper in a separate large bowl or large plastic food bag.

Soy sauce, garlic chile paste, ketchup, honey, apricot preserves, red bell pepper, scallions, and rice wine should all be combined in a blender. Blend until thoroughly combined.

Pour the sauce mixture into a large saucepan and heat over medium heat, stirring frequently, for 5 minutes, or until the sauce begins to thicken. Reduce the heat to low and continue to cook, stirring occasionally.

In a large, deep frying pan or deep fryer, heat 1-2 inches of vegetable oil over medium-high heat.

Place the chicken in the cornstarch and toss to coat in small batches.

Once the oil is hot, place the chicken pieces in the oil with tongs and fry until golden brown, about 2-3 minutes per side. Remove from the pan and set aside to drain some of the oil.

Return the chicken pieces to the hot oil for another 2-3 minutes, lightly dusting with cornstarch. Remove the chicken from the oil and set aside to drain.

Pour the warm sauce over the chicken in a large mixing bowl. To coat evenly, toss.

Serve right away.

Fish Balls with Spicy Sauce

10 minutes to prepare

Preparation Time: 15 minutes

6 servings

12-pound cod or whitefish fillet, cubed 12-pound shrimp, cleaned and deveined, chopped 12 cups sweet yellow onion, celery, carrots, peeled and chopped tablespoon chile pepper, diced garlic cloves

1 tablespoon chopped fresh chives

1 teaspoon black pepper 1 teaspoon salt

12 tsp cayenne powder 12 tsp fresh lemongrass 12 tsp sugar 12 tsp rice wine

14 cup flour 1 egg 1 tablespoon cornstarch

Fryable vegetable oil

In a food processor, combine the cod and shrimp and pulse until finely ground. Set aside after removing from the food processor.

In the food processor, combine the onion, celery, carrots, chile pepper, garlic, and chives. Pulse until well combined and ground.

In a mixing bowl, combine the seafood and vegetable mixtures.

Season with salt, black pepper, cayenne pepper, and lemongrass. Combine thoroughly.

Dissolve the sugar in the rice wine and combine it with the egg, cornstarch, and flour. Mix until everything is well combined. The mixture should be thick enough to form balls but still be slightly sticky to the touch.

In a large frying pan, heat 1-2 inches of vegetable oil over high heat. Reduce the heat to medium once the oil is hot.

Scoop out balls of the fish mixture with a small ice cream scoop or a spoon. Cook until golden brown, approximately 2-3 minutes per side, in the oil.

Remove from the pan and allow the excess oil to drain.

Serve immediately, either plain or with your preferred dipping sauce.

Mandu served with a simple sesame dipping sauce (Korean Dumplings)

15 minutes to prepare

Preparation Time: 15 minutes

6-8 people

12-pound ground pork is used in this recipe.

3 tbsp vegetable or peanut oil (divided)

14 cups red onion, diced 12 cup cabbage, shredded 12 cup carrot, shredded tablespoon fresh ginger, grated 14 cups scallions, diced 12-pound tofu, mashed tablespoons hoisin sauce

1 teaspoon black pepper 1 teaspoon salt

24 wonton skins, large

1 lightly beaten egg

Extra vegetable oil for frying

Sauce

12 c. soy sauce

14 cups of rice vinegar

2 tsp white sugar 2 tsp sesame oil tablespoon diced chile pepper 2 tsp sesame seeds

In a large skillet or wok, heat 1 tablespoon of the peanut or vegetable oil over medium heat. Cook until the ground pork is browned, taking care to break it up into small pieces as it cooks.

Remove the meat from the pan once it has browned and set it aside.

Heat the remaining oil in the pan over medium-high heat.

Mix in the garlic and onion. Before adding the cabbage and carrots, sauté for 2 minutes. Cook for 3 minutes more, stirring constantly.

After that, stir in the ginger, scallions, mashed tofu, and hoisin sauce. Cook for another 2-3 minutes before removing from the pan and mixing with the browned pork.

After the pan has cooled, wipe it out and add 12-1 inch of vegetable oil to it. Warm the oil over medium-high heat.

While the oil is heating, make the sauce by combining the soy sauce, rice vinegar, sugar, sesame oil, chile pepper, and sesame seeds. Set aside after thoroughly whisking.

Brush the outer edges of 1 or 2 wonton skins with the beaten egg on a flat surface. Cover the remaining skins to prevent them from drying out.

Place a heaping spoonful of the meat mixture in the wonton, slightly off-center.

Fold the wonton skins in half and press the edges together to form a triangle. Check that the edges are sealed, and crimp them if desired.

Place the dumpling in the hot oil in the pan. Cook for 2-3 minutes per side, or until golden brown.

Remove from the pan and set aside to drain any excess oil.

Serve immediately with prepared dipping sauce.

Hello, Muchim (Spicy Cucumber Salad)

Cooking Time: 0

Preparation Time: 20 minutes

4 people

4 cups pickling cucumbers, sliced approximately 14-inch thick

1 tbsp coarsely ground salt

1 tablespoon vinegar (rice)

1 teaspoon of white sugar

1 tbsp garlic-chile paste

14 cups scallions 1 cup sweet yellow onion, thinly sliced

1 tablespoon toasted sesame seeds

Place the sliced cucumbers in a large mixing bowl and season with coarse ground salt. Toss everything together and set aside for 15-20 minutes.

Place the cucumbers in a colander and thoroughly rinse to remove the salt. Pat dry the cucumber slices with a soft cloth or paper towel on a flat surface. For the crispest salad, remove as much moisture as possible.

Combine the rice vinegar, white sugar, and garlic chile paste in the large bowl that the cucumbers were originally in. Whisk thoroughly.

Toss the onions and cucumbers in the bowl to coat.

Toss in the scallions and sesame seeds one or two more times to evenly distribute them throughout the salad.

Refrigerate the salad for 30 minutes before serving.

If used within 24 hours, it is best.

Soup with Rice Cakes

30 minutes to prepare

Preparation Time: 15 minutes

6-8 people

2 pounds of prepared Korean rice cake rounds, plus cold water for soaking

1 tbsp. vegetable oil

12 cups diced yellow onion

3 crushed and minced garlic cloves

12lb ground beef 1 teaspoon sea salt

1 teaspoon ground black pepper 14 tbsp soy sauce

1 teaspoon of fish sauce

8 cups beef stock (low sodium)

1 tbsp sesame oil

1 teaspoon rice wine

Garnish

14 cups diced scallions

Strips of omelet

Sesame seeds for decoration

Fill a bowl halfway with cold water and add the prepared rice cakes. Allow sitting for 15 minutes, or until softened.

In a soup pot, heat the oil over medium heat. Mix in the onion and garlic. Cook for 3 minutes.

Brown the ground beef, taking care to break it up into small pieces as you cook, for about 5-7 minutes. Season with salt and black pepper and drain any excess grease.

Combine the soy sauce, fish sauce, beef stock, sesame oil, and rice wine in a mixing bowl. Combine thoroughly. Bring the broth to a low boil over high heat. Reduce the heat to low, cover, and leave to cook for 15-20 minutes.

If you haven't already, remove the rice cakes from the cold water and place them in individual serving bowls. Fill each bowl with some of the crumbled seaweed.

Ladle the soup into the bowls and set aside for a few minutes to soften the seaweed before serving.

Garnish with sliced scallions, sesame seeds, and omelet strips if desired.

Soup with Fermented Soybean and Shrimp

Time to cook: 25 minutes

Preparation Time: 10 minutes

4 people

1 tablespoon of either peanut or vegetable oil

1 cup diced red onion

1 cup shredded carrot 3 crushed and minced garlic cloves

1 cup sliced zucchini

a dozen bean sprouts

1 cup cleaned and deveined shrimp, chopped

4 cups water or fish stock

1 teaspoon of fish sauce

12 cups fermented soy paste 1 cup cubed firm tofu

1 tablespoon chopped fresh chives

In a soup pot, heat the peanut or vegetable oil over medium heat.

Sauté the red onion for 3 minutes.

After that, add the carrot and garlic. Cook for 3 minutes more, stirring constantly.

Combine the zucchini and bean sprouts in a mixing bowl. Cook for another 2-3 minutes.

Toss the shrimp lightly in the pot before adding the fish stock or water, fish sauce, and fermented soybean paste. Bring to a low boil after thoroughly mixing.

Reduce the heat to low and stir in the tofu. Before serving, cover and simmer for 15 minutes.

Garnish with fresh chives before serving.

YukGaejang (Spicy Beef Soup) (Spicy Beef Soup)

30 minutes to prepare

Preparation Time: 10 minutes

6-8 people

12-pound beef roast or brisket, cooked and shredded

1 tbsp. vegetable oil

12 cups diced onion

4 crushed and minced garlic cloves

1 tablespoon diced chile pepper

1 tablespoon grated fresh ginger

3 cups shredded cabbage

2 tbsp sesame seed oil

1 tbsp fiery red pepper paste

14 cup soy sauce 8 cups beef broth

1 tbsp lime juice

beaten eggs

Serve with cooked rice or noodles.

In a soup pot, heat the vegetable oil over medium-high heat.

Cook for 3 minutes after adding the onion.

Add the garlic, chile pepper, and ginger next. Cook, stirring constantly, for 2-3 minutes, or until the mixture is fragrant.

Season the cabbage with sesame oil and spicy red pepper paste. Cook for 3-4 minutes, or until the cabbage starts to wilt.

Cover the shredded beef with the beef broth, soy sauce, and lime juice in a pot. Bring to a low boil before lowering the heat to low, covering, and allowing the soup to simmer for 15-20 minutes.

Remove the lid from the pot and gradually drizzle in the beaten egg, whisking the entire time to ensure even distribution.

Place the rice or noodles in separate serving bowls before ladling the hot soup on top.

Jjigae Kimchi (Kimchi Stew)

30 minutes to prepare

Preparation Time: 15 minutes

2-4 people

1 pound of skinless pork belly, thinly sliced

4 crushed and minced garlic cloves

14 cups rice wine 1 tablespoon grated fresh ginger

1 tablespoon vegetable oil 1 cup thinly sliced yellow onion 1 cup kimchi, liquid drained and reserved

12 cups sliced shiitake mushrooms 2 cups fish stock cup kimchi liquid tablespoons soy sauce

1 tbsp. red chile pastes

a tbsp fermented bean paste

1 tablespoon red pepper flakes, crushed

12-pound cubed tofu

Scallions, sliced, for garnish

In a mixing bowl, combine the garlic, ginger, and rice wine. Whisk everything together.

Toss the pork belly in the bowl to coat. Allow it to marinate for about 15-20 minutes.

In a soup pot, heat the vegetable oil over medium heat. Combine the onions and drained kimchi in a mixing bowl. Cook, stirring constantly, for 3-5 minutes, or until the kimchi softens.

Cook, stirring constantly, for 5-7 minutes, or until the sliced pork belly begins to brown slightly.

Cook for an additional 1-2 minutes after adding the mushrooms.

Cover with the kimchi liquid, fish stock, and soy sauce. Combine thoroughly.

Combine the red chile paste, fermented bean paste, and crushed red pepper in a mixing bowl.

Increase the heat to medium-high and cook the soup until it reaches a low boil.

Reduce the heat to low and cook for 20-25 minutes.

If desired, garnish with sliced scallions.

Noodles, Pancakes, and Rice

Pancakes with Mung Beans

15 minutes to prepare

Preparation Time: 15 minutes

4-6 people

1 cup peeled mung beans, soaked for at least 4 hours or overnight

1 cup vegetable stock or water

egg, lightly beaten

2 teaspoons flour

1 tablespoon chopped fresh chives

12 teaspoons of salt

1 cup cleaned and trimmed green beans

1 cup thickly shredded carrots and a dozen bean sprouts

1 cup scallions, thinly sliced

Cooking oil from vegetables

Drain the mung beans and put them in a food processor or blender.

Combine the water or vegetable stock, crushed red pepper flakes, eggs, flour, chives, and salt in a mixing bowl. Pulse until the batter is smooth and pourable.

Combine the green beans, carrots, bean sprouts, and scallions in a mixing bowl. Toss to combine.

Mix the batter into the vegetables thoroughly.

Brush a skillet liberally with vegetable oil and heat over medium-high heat.

Fill the pan with a large scoop of pancake batter. Cook for 2-3 minutes, or until the edges turn golden brown, before flipping and cooking for another 1-2 minutes.

Remove from the heat and keep warm while you finish the remaining batter.

Warm with your favorite dipping sauce, and serve.

Pancakes with Kimchi

15 minutes to prepare

Preparation Time: 10 minutes

4 people

Ingredients:

1 cup kimchi, drained with reserved liquid

14 cups sliced radish 14 cups sliced scallions

1 teaspoon red pepper flakes, crushed

12 cups liquid kimchi cup whole wheat flour eggs

Cooking oil from vegetables

Combine the drained kimchi, radish, scallions, and crushed red pepper flakes in a mixing bowl. Toss to combine.

In a separate bowl, combine the kimchi liquid, whole wheat flour, and eggs. Mix until the eggs are completely incorporated.

Stir the batter into the kimchi mixture.

Brush a skillet liberally with vegetable oil and heat over medium-high heat.

Spoon a ladle of batter onto the skillet and gently press down. Cook for about 2-3 minutes, or until the edges start to turn golden brown.

Cook for another 2 minutes after flipping the pancake.

Remove the pancake from the pan and set aside while you finish the rest of the batter.

Warm with your favorite dipping sauce, and serve.

Pancakes with Sesame Vegetables

15 minutes to prepare

Preparation Time: 15 minutes

4 people

2 cups zucchini, shredded cup carrots, shredded cup napa cabbage, shredded12 cups scallions, sliced 2 garlic cloves, crushed and minced

12 tsp salt 1 tsp Korean soy sauce

1 tbsp sesame oil

2 tsp sesame seeds, toasted

12 cup water 12 cups flour 12 cups eggs

Cooking oil from vegetables

Place the zucchini in a colander and squeeze out as much liquid as possible. Combine it with the carrots, napa cabbage, scallions, and garlic in a mixing bowl. Toss to combine.

Season with salt, Korean soy sauce, sesame oil, and sesame seeds to taste. Combine thoroughly.

To make a batter, combine the flour, water, and eggs in a separate bowl. Toss the vegetables in the batter to coat.

Brush a skillet liberally with vegetable oil and heat over medium-high heat.

Spoon a ladle of batter onto the skillet and gently press down. Cook for about 2-3 minutes, or until the edges start to turn golden brown.

Cook for another 2 minutes after flipping the pancake.

Remove it from the pan and set it aside while you finish the rest of the batter.

Warm with your favorite dipping sauce, and serve.

Pancakes with Seafood

Time to cook: 20 minutes

Preparation Time: 10 minutes

4 people

1 cup flour and 12 cup cornstarch

12 teaspoons black pepper 12 teaspoons salt

1 tablespoon chopped fresh chives

2 cups asparagus spears, chopped 1 cup scallions, sliced thick cup orange bell pepper, sliced cloves garlic, crushed and minced 12-pound shrimp, cleaned and deveined, chopped 12-pound whitefish fillets, cut into small cubes

In a mixing bowl, combine the flour, cornstarch, salt, black pepper, and chives. Combine thoroughly.

To make a thin pancake batter, combine the egg and water. Set aside after thoroughly mixing.

In a large skillet over medium heat, heat half of the vegetable oil.

Combine the asparagus, scallions, and orange bell pepper in a mixing bowl. Cook for 3 minutes while stirring.

Cook for 1 minute more after adding the garlic. Set aside the vegetables after they have been removed from the pan.

Sauté the shrimp and white fish in the pan for 5-6 minutes, or until cooked through. Remove from the pan and add the vegetables.

Brush the skillet liberally with the remaining vegetable oil.

Spread one-quarter of the vegetable and fish mixture evenly in the pan.

Pour one-quarter of the batter over the vegetables and fish, swirling the skillet to distribute the batter evenly and creating a thin pancake.

Cook for 2-3 minutes, or until the edges start to brown.

Flip the pancake carefully and cook for another 2 minutes.

Remove from the heat and keep warm while you work through the remaining ingredients.

Serve warm with your favorite dipping sauce, and cut into quarters.

Traditional Bibimbap

Time to cook: 35-40 minutes

Preparation Time: 15 minutes

6 people

Ingredients: \sBulgogi

1 pound thinly sliced beef steak 12 c. soy sauce

14 cups shredded Asian pear

3 crushed and minced garlic cloves

14 cups Asian pears 14 c. rice wine

three tbsp white sugar

1 tablespoon grated fresh ginger

1 tablespoon toasted sesame seeds

1 teaspoon black pepper, coarse

Rice

6 cups cooked sushi rice 1 tbsp toasted sesame seeds 2 tbsp sesame oil

Vegetables

3 cups shredded carrots

1 tablespoon grated fresh ginger

6 cups fresh spinach garlic cloves, crushed and minced tbsp soy sauce

two tbsp rice vinegar

2 cups sliced shiitake mushrooms

1-quart beef broth 1 tbsp brown sugar

1 tbsp. red pepper paste

4 cups mung bean sprouts, cooked 14 cup sesame oil, 6 eggs divided

Begin by preparing the marinade for the bulgogi. Combine the soy sauce, Asian pear, garlic, Asian pear juice, rice wine, white sugar, ginger, sesame seeds, and black pepper in a large mixing bowl. Combine thoroughly.

Toss the meat in the marinade to coat. Refrigerate for at least 30 minutes, covered.

Combine the rice and sesame seeds in a mixing bowl. Combine thoroughly.

Spread the sesame oil around in a skillet, using a brush if necessary. Heat over medium heat.

Add the rice and gently press it into the pan. Cook for 12-15 minutes, pressing occasionally, until the bottom of the rice begins to brown and crisp.

Cook for an additional 3-5 minutes, stirring occasionally with a spatula.

Combine the shredded carrots, ginger, and 1 tablespoon of sesame oil in a mixing bowl. Set aside after thoroughly mixing.

In a saucepan, bring 3 cups of water to a boil. Cook for 1-2 minutes in boiling water with the spinach. Press out as much moisture as possible from the spinach.

In a sauté pan, combine 1 tablespoon of sesame oil, spinach, garlic, soy sauce, and rice vinegar. Cook for 3 minutes on medium heat. Set aside after removing from the pan.

Combine the sliced shiitake mushrooms, beef broth, brown sugar, and red pepper paste in a saucepan. Bring to a boil, then reduce to low heat and leave to cook for 5-7 minutes.

Cook the meat in a skillet over medium heat until it reaches the desired doneness, about 7-10 minutes.

Set the meat aside after removing it from the pan. Fry each egg until the yolk has reached the desired consistency.

Divide the crisp rice among six serving bowls.

Arrange the meat, carrots, spinach, mushrooms, and mung bean sprouts in small individual piles over the rice in each dish.

Before serving, top each dish with a fried egg.

Bokkeumbap (Kimchi Fried Rice) (Kimchi Fried Rice)

Time to cook: 25 minutes

Preparation Time: 10 minutes

4 people

2 cups kimchi, chopped 12-pound pork belly, thinly sliced 14 cups daikon, shredded 3 cups cooked rice

14 cups liquid kimchi

1 teaspoon red pepper flakes, crushed

1 tbsp sesame oil

4 eggs

Scallions, sliced for decoration

Cook the pork belly in a skillet over medium to medium-high heat until it is browned, about 5 minutes.

Cook for 3 minutes more after adding the daikon.

Take the pork belly and daikon out of the pan and set aside.

Take out all but about 1 tablespoon of the pork fat from the skillet.

Cook, stirring constantly, until the kimchi is tender, about 5 minutes.

Add the rice and gently press it into the pan's bottom. Cook for another 7-10 minutes, stirring occasionally.

Before adding the pork belly, season the rice with the kimchi liquid and sesame oil.

Toss everything together and keep it warm over low heat.

Meanwhile, lightly oil another skillet and fry each egg until the yolk is done to preference.

Divide the rice between four individual serving plates and top with a fried egg on each.

If desired, garnish with sliced scallions.

The fiery DukBokki (Korean Rice Cakes)

10 minutes to prepare

Preparation Time: 10 minutes

4-6 people

8 long sticky rice cake sticks, cooked according to package directions if refrigerated 14 cups Korean soy sauce 1 tablespoon vegetable oil 14 cups hot chile paste

12 tsp white sugar 12 tsp rice vinegar

1 tbsp sesame oil

1 tablespoon chopped fresh lemongrass

Cut the sticky rice cake sticks into 1-inch pieces.

Heat the vegetable oil in a large skillet over medium heat.

Combine the Korean soy sauce, spicy chile paste, white sugar, rice vinegar, and sesame oil in a mixing bowl. Combine thoroughly.

Cook the rice cakes in the hot skillet until lightly browned all over, about 5-7 minutes.

Pour the prepared sauce into the skillet and toss to coat for 2 minutes more.

Before serving, remove from the pan and garnish with fresh lemongrass.

Serve immediately.

Chae Jap (Korean Glass Noodles)

15 minutes to prepare

Preparation Time: 10 minutes

2-4 people

12-pound sirloin steak, thinly sliced 12-pound glass noodles, cooked 1 tablespoon vegetable oil cup onion, sliced cloves garlic, crushed and minced 1 cup carrot, shredded 1 cup scallions, sliced thick cup oyster mushrooms, sliced cups fresh spinach

14 tbsp soy sauce

a tbsp. sesame oil

2 tbsp. sesame seeds

In a large skillet or wok, heat the vegetable oil over medium-high heat.

Cook for 2-3 minutes, or until the steak is cooked through. Set aside after removing from the wok.

If necessary, add oil and sauté the onion and garlic for 1-2 minutes.

Turn the heat down to medium. Combine the carrots, scallions, and mushrooms in a mixing bowl. Cook for another 4-5 minutes.

Add the spinach and black pepper to taste. Cook for 1 minute, or until the spinach is wilted.

Drizzle soy sauce and sesame oil over the cooked noodles in the pan. Toss to combine. Cook for 3 minutes, stirring gently.

Toss with the sesame seeds right before serving.

Stir-Fry Sesame Seed Sweet Potato Glass Noodles

Time to cook: 20 minutes

Preparation Time: 10 minutes

2-4 people

4 cups fresh spinach, chopped cup kimchi cabbage cloves 1 tablespoon vegetable oil cups green beans, trimmed 1 cup scallions, sliced thick crushed and minced garlic

12 teaspoon salt 2 cups sliced shiitake mushrooms

14 cups Korean soy sauce 1 teaspoon black pepper 1 tsp. lime juice

1 tbsp brown sugar 1 tsp crushed red pepper flakes

a tbsp. sesame oil

12 pounds thinly sliced beef steak

1 tablespoon black or golden sesame seeds

12-pound cooked sweet potato glass noodles

In a large skillet or wok heat the vegetable oil over medium heat.

Combine the green beans and scallions in a mixing bowl. Cook for 4-5 minutes.

Add the spinach, cabbage, garlic, and mushrooms next. Sauté the mushrooms for 3-4 minutes, or until tender. Season the vegetables with salt and black pepper before removing them from the pan and setting them aside.

Combine the Korean soy sauce, lime juice, brown sugar, and crushed red pepper flakes in a mixing bowl. To combine, whisk everything together.

Cook the sesame oil and beef in the skillet for 5-7 minutes, or until done to preference.

During the last minute of cooking the beef, add the sesame seeds to the pan.

Reduce the heat to low and return the vegetables to the skillet. Toss to combine.

Finally, add the noodles to the pan and toss them around until they are heated through.

Serve right away.

Guksu, Bibim (Spicy Cold Noodles)

10 minutes to prepare

Preparation Time: 10 minutes

4 people

1 pound soba noodles 14 cup rice vinegar 14 cups white sugar tablespoons Korean soy sauce

1 tbsp sesame oil

14 cups fiery chile paste tsp crushed red pepper flakes

1 tablespoon toasted sesame seeds

1 cup chopped kimchi 12 cups thinly sliced Korean radish

1 cup matchstick-cut pickling cucumber

1 cup thinly sliced napa cabbage 12 cup bean sprouts Scallions, sliced for garnish

Cook the soba noodles according to package directions, then shock them in cold water. If necessary, drizzle a little sesame oil over the noodles to keep them from sticking.

Combine the rice vinegar, white sugar, Korean soy sauce, sesame oil, spicy chile paste, and crushed red pepper flakes in a mixing bowl. Combine thoroughly.

Arrange the soba noodles in neat piles in the center of the serving plates.

Drizzle the sauce over the noodles and sprinkle with sesame seeds.

Next, arrange the kimchi, radish, cucumber, cabbage, and bean sprouts around the noodles.

Alternately, combine the vegetables and arrange them on serving plates, followed by noodles, sauce, sesame seeds, and kimchi.

If desired, garnish with scallions before serving

Noodles with Black Bean Sauce

30 minutes to prepare

Preparation Time: 10 minutes

4-6 people

1 pound pork tenderloin, cut into cubes 3 tablespoons rice wine

14 teaspoon salt 12 teaspoons black pepper 2 garlic cloves, crushed and minced tablespoon fresh ginger, grated Soba noodles 1 pound 14 cup olive oil

12 cups pureed black beans

2 tbsp brown sugar or honey 1 tbsp rice vinegar 2 tsp fish sauce

1 cup sliced onion 1 cup sweet potatoes cubed cup zucchini sliced cups napa cabbage shredded

1 tablespoon cornstarch 2 cups chicken or vegetable stock

Season the pork in a bowl with the rice wine, garlic, ginger, salt, and black pepper. Refrigerate for at least 30 minutes, covered.

Soba noodles should be cooked according to package directions.

In a large skillet or wok, heat the vegetable oil over medium heat.

Combine the black bean paste with brown sugar or honey. Cook for 5 minutes, stirring constantly.

Cook for another 2 minutes after adding the rice vinegar and fish sauce.

Cook, stirring frequently until the pork is browned in the skillet or wok.

Add the onion and sweet potato cubes next. Cook for another 5 minutes, or until they start to soften.

Cook, stirring constantly, for 3 minutes after adding the zucchini and cabbage.

To the skillet, add everything except 14 cups of chicken stock.

Mix the remaining 14 cups with the cornstarch until no lumps remain.

For 5 minutes, increase the heat to medium-high before lowering it to medium-low.

Mix in the cornstarch mixture thoroughly. Simmer for 10 minutes, covered.

Serve immediately over (or alongside) cooked soba noodles.

Bulgogi

15 minutes to prepare

Preparation Time: 10 minute

4-6 people

Ingredients:

12-pound sirloin or another tender steak, thinly sliced

12 cup soy sauce (Korean)

14 cups granulated sugar

2 tbsp. rice wine

2 crushed and minced garlic cloves

2 teaspoons grated fresh ginger

14 cup pineapple, finely diced, or thinly sliced Asian pear

12 teaspoons salt1 teaspoon coarse ground black pepper

14 teaspoon cayenne pepper powder (optional)

a tbsp. sesame oil

1 cup sliced sweet yellow onion

12 cups julienned carrot

12 cups sliced leeks

1 tablespoon sesame seeds, toasted

Serve with lettuce leaves (optional)

Serve with rice (optional)

1 sliced green onion for garnish

Directions:

Combine the Korean soy sauce, brown sugar, rice wine, garlic, ginger, pineapple, black pepper, salt, and cayenne in a blender. Blend until completely smooth.

Mix the marinade into the sliced meat in an airtight container or resealable plastic bag. Place the meat in the refrigerator for 2-4 hours, covered.

In a skillet or wok, heat the sesame oil over medium-high heat.

To the skillet, add the meat, along with any remaining marinade, as well as the onion, carrot, and leek.

Cook, stirring frequently, for 5 minutes, or until the meat begins to brown.

Reduce the heat to medium and cook until the meat is done and the vegetables are crisp-tender.

Reduce the heat to low, then add the sesame seeds and cook for 1 minute more.

If desired, serve with lettuce leaves and rice.

Before serving, top with green onions.

Korean Beef Tacos in the Slow Cooker

8 hours to cook

Preparation Time: 10 minutes

6-8 people

Ingredients:

2 pounds roast beef

14 cups brown sugar 12 cups Korean soy sauce

14 cups shredded apple 1 tablespoon spicy chile paste

1 tablespoon vinegar (rice)

1 cup sliced onion

1 cup chopped kimchi

14 cups sliced Korean radish

To serve, use lettuce leaves or tortillas.

Directions:

In a slow cooker, place the roast beef.

In a mixing bowl, combine the Korean soy sauce, brown sugar, spicy chile paste, apple, and rice vinegar. Mix thoroughly and pour over the

meat.

Insert the onion into the slow cooker. Set the slow cooker to low and cover it. Cook for 8 hours, or until the potatoes are tender.

When the meat is done cooking, shred it and return it to the slow cooker with the onions and any cooking liquid.

Serve the meat on lettuce leaves or tortillas, topped with kimchi and sliced Korean radish

Beef with Sticky Scallions

15 minutes to prepare

Time to prepare: 10 minutes plus marinade time

4 people

Ingredients:

1 pound sliced beef steak

14 cups plus 2 tablespoons soy sauce

1 teaspoon rice wine

1 tsp sesame oil

2 tbsp cornstarch, divided (plus additional for coating the beef)

14 cups brown sugar 4 tbsp water

12 cup beef stock

3 tablespoons olive oil

1 tablespoon sliced chile pepper

3 crushed and minced garlic cloves

2 teaspoons grated fresh ginger

1 tablespoon chopped chives

6-8 trimmed and sliced green onions, lengthwise or diagonally

Serve with cooked rice

Directions:

2 tablespoons soy sauce, rice wine, and sesame oil, plus 1-2 teaspoons cornstarch Combine thoroughly.

Coat the meat with the marinade mixture in a bowl. Refrigerate for 1 to 3 hours, covered.

In a separate bowl, whisk together the remaining cornstarch and water until no lumps remain.

Add the brown sugar and beef broth to the cornstarch. Set aside after thoroughly mixing.

Remove the meat from the marinade and lightly coat it with cornstarch.

In a large skillet or wok, heat the vegetable oil over medium-high heat. Cook the meat in the skillet until it is browned and crispy on both sides, about 1-2 minutes per side. Set the meat aside after removing it from the pan.

To the skillet, add the chile pepper, garlic, ginger, chives, and scallions. Cook until the mixture is fragrant, about 1-2 minutes.

Pour in the prepared sauce and cook, stirring frequently, for 3-5 minutes, or until the sauce thickens.

Cook for 1-2 minutes after adding the meat to the pan.

If desired, serve immediately with cooked rice.

Gochujang Glazed Meatballs

Time to cook: 25 minutes

Preparation Time: 10 minutes

4 people

Ingredients:

1 pound beef ground

3 crushed and minced garlic cloves

12 cups shredded carrots

14 cups shredded Asian pear

2 teaspoons chopped fresh chives

1 tablespoon chile paste, spicy

12 cup panko or bread crumbs

1 egg

1 teaspoon sea salt

1 teaspoon ground black pepper

1 tbsp. vegetable oil

Glaze with Gochujang

3 tbsp. spicy chile paste (Gochujang)

2 tablespoons rice vinegar 12 cup strawberry preserves

1 teaspoon grated fresh ginger

1 teaspoon soy sauce

tsp crushed red pepper flakes (optional)

1 tablespoon sesame seeds, toasted

Scallions, sliced for decoration

Directions:

Preheat the oven to 350 degrees Fahrenheit and line a baking sheet with parchment paper.

Combine the ground beef, garlic, carrots, Asian pear, chives, and spicy chile paste in a mixing bowl. Combine thoroughly.

Combine the panko or other bread crumbs with the egg. Season with salt and black pepper to taste. Mix well with your hands to distribute the egg and breadcrumbs evenly.

In a large skillet over medium heat, heat the vegetable oil.

Form the meat mixture into balls about 12 inches in diameter, taking care not to overwork the meat.

Brown the meatballs evenly on all sides of the pan. Remove the meatballs from the pan and place them on the prepared baking sheet.

Bake for 15 minutes, or until thoroughly cooked.

In a saucepan, combine the Gochujang, strawberry preserves, rice vinegar, ginger, soy sauce, red pepper flakes, and sesame seeds while the meatballs are cooking. Cook, stirring frequently, until all of the ingredients are well combined and slightly thickened, about 5-7 minutes.

Remove the meatballs from the oven and toss them in the glaze while they are still hot.

Serve immediately, if desired garnished with fresh scallions.

Chicken Fried in Korean Style

Time to cook: 25 minutes

Preparation Time: 10 minutes

4-6 people

Ingredients:

2 pounds chicken legs (skinned if desired)

1/4 cup flour

a 12 cup rice flour

12 teaspoons of salt

1 tsp coarsely ground black pepper

12 teaspoons cayenne pepper 12 teaspoon garlic powder 2 lightly beaten eggs

12 cups soy sauce12 cup vegetable oil

14 cups ketchup (tomato)

2 crushed and minced garlic cloves

1 tablespoon hot chile paste

2 tsp hot mustard

1 teaspoon honey

1 tablespoon vinegar (rice)

Directions:

Combine the flour, rice flour, salt, black pepper, cayenne pepper powder, and garlic powder in a mixing bowl. Combine thoroughly.

Dredge each piece of chicken through the flour mixture.

Set aside after dipping each piece of chicken in the beaten egg and then again in the flour mixture.

Heat the vegetable oil in a large frying pan over medium-high heat.

Place the chicken legs in the pan once the oil is hot and cook, turning occasionally until the chicken is a deep golden brown and crispy, about 15-20 minutes depending on the size of the pieces.

Combine the soy sauce, ketchup, garlic, chile paste, hot mustard, honey, and rice vinegar while the chicken is cooking. Cook for at least 5 minutes over medium heat, stirring frequently.

When the chicken is done, remove it from the pan and drain any excess cooking oil.

Brush the chicken with the still-warm sauce with a basting brush.

Serve right away.

Dakkochi (Skewered Chicken) (Skewered Chicken)

10 minutes to prepare

Preparation Time: 15 minutes

6 people

Ingredients:

2 pounds cubed boneless skinless chicken breast

12 c. soy sauce

1 tbsp sesame seed oil

1 teaspoon honey

14 cup apple, shredded 1 tablespoon fresh ginger, grated

4 crushed and minced garlic cloves

12 teaspoons of salt

1 teaspoon ground black pepper

10 green onions, cut into 1-inch pieces

Directions:

In a mixing bowl, combine the soy sauce, sesame oil, honey, ginger, apple, garlic, salt, and black pepper. Combine thoroughly.

Place the chicken in the bowl, toss to coat, cover, and chill for at least 4-6 hours.

Soak bamboo skewers in water before using them.

Set up and preheat an indoor or outdoor grill.

Place the chicken pieces on prepared bamboo or metal skewers. Alternate with 2-3 green onion slices.

Grill the skewers until they are cooked through, about 5-6 minutes per side.

Cornish Hens with Ginseng

1.5 hours to cook

Preparation Time: 15 minutes

3-4 people

Ingredients:

2 hens from Cornwall

1 tbsp. vegetable oil

1 tsp coarse sea salt

1 teaspoon ground black pepper

1 cup sticky rice, soaked in water overnight

1 cup red Korean dates

8 whole garlic cloves

2 to 4 chestnuts

5 cup chicken broth

1-inch fresh ginger, peeled

2 whole carrots, peeled and halved

2 ginseng roots, dried

Directions:

After washing and patting the hens dry, brush them with vegetable oil and season with salt and black pepper.

Drain the sweet rice thoroughly and divide it evenly among the Cornish hen cavities.

Inside each hen, place 1 or 2 dates, 2 garlic cloves, and the chestnuts. Tie each hen with kitchen twine to keep the rice securely in place.

Bring the chicken stock, ginger, carrots, remaining garlic, dates, and ginseng root to a boil in a stock pot.

Place the hens in the broth and return it to a gentle boil. Reduce to low heat and cover for 1 hour and 15 minutes.

Remove the hens from the broth and set them aside for 10 minutes to rest.

Serve the hens whole or cut in half in bowls of ginseng broth.

Sandwiches with pulled pork and a cucumber-scallion salad

8 hours to cook

Preparation Time: 15 minutes

8 people

Ingredients:

Tenderloin of pork, about 2 pounds

12 cups hot chile paste

14 c. hoisin sauce

12 c. soy sauce

12 cup ketchup (tomato)

2 teaspoon honey

12 cup chicken stock 2 tablespoons Asian pear juice

8 crushed and minced garlic cloves

1 cup sliced onion

pods of star anise

1 cup sliced cucumber

12 cups sliced scallions 1 cup rice vinegar

12 cups granulated sugar

tsp crushed red pepper flakes

1 tsp coarse sea salt

Serve with buns

Directions:

In a slow cooker, place the tenderloin.

Combine the chile paste, hoisin sauce, soy sauce, tomato ketchup, honey, Asian pear juice, and chicken stock in a mixing bowl. Pour the mixture over the tenderloin and mix well.

Crush the garlic, slice the onion, and add the star anise pods. Cook on low for 8 hours, covered.

In a mixing bowl, combine the cucumbers and scallions. Combine the rice vinegar, white sugar, red pepper flakes, and salt in a mixing bowl. Pour over the cucumbers after thoroughly mixing. To combine, stir everything together. Refrigerate for at least 2 hours, covered.

Remove the meat from the slow cooker once it is cooked through and tender.

Pour the cooking liquid into a saucepan and heat over medium heat for 5-10 minutes, stirring occasionally. Take out the star anise.

Shred the pork and stir it into the pan sauce.

Serve on buns with pickled cucumbers and scallions on top.

Dumplings with Steamed Pork

Time to cook: 25 minutes

Time to prepare: 30 minutes plus rest time

4-6 people

Ingredients:

2 c. flour

14 cups water 1 teaspoon dry yeast

12-pound pork ground

1 tablespoon diced chile pepper

2 tbsp. soy sauce

2 tbsp of rice wine

2 crushed and minced garlic cloves

14 cups sliced scallions

1 cup chopped kimchee

Directions:

In a mixing bowl, combine the flour and yeast. After that, slowly pour in the water and mix it in with the flour. Use your hands or another gentle method to mix the dough, being careful not to overwork it. If necessary, add more flour to make a soft but slightly sticky dough.

Flour a flat surface as well as your hands. Remove the dough from the bowl and knead it with your hands until it feels springy, adding flour as needed. Form the dough into a ball and return it to the bowl.

Cover the bowl with a damp towel and leave it out for 3 hours to rest and rise.

In a skillet, combine the ground pork, chile pepper, soy sauce, rice wine, garlic, and scallions. Cook, stirring frequently, for 7-10 minutes, or until the pork is browned.

Take the pork off the heat and combine it with the chopped kimchi.

Remove the dough from the bowl and re-flour your work surface and hands.

Make 12 equal-sized balls out of the dough. Roll each ball into a flat circle about 4 inches in diameter.

Fill each circle with a generous spoonful of the pork mixture.

Pull the dough up like a purse around the filling. Crimp the top shut in a circular pattern.

Cover and set aside for 10-15 minutes.

In a pot of hot water, prepare a steaming rack. Use parchment paper to line the steaming rack. A bamboo steamer can also be used.

Arrange the dumplings on parchment paper. Cook for 12-15 minutes, covered, over gently boiling water.

Remove from the steaming water and serve hot.

Squid with Spicy Vegetables

10 minutes to prepare

Preparation Time: 10 minutes

4 people

Soy sauce (three tablespoons)

1 tablespoon chile paste, spicy

1 tbsp sesame oil

14 cups fish stock tablespoon brown sugar teaspoons fresh lemongrass, chopped

1 tbsp. vegetable oil 12 cups thinly sliced carrot 12 cup onion, diced 12 cups mushrooms, sliced 4 small squids, cleaned and sliced 1 teaspoon sesame seeds for garnish

Serve with rice

Combine the soy sauce, chile paste, sesame oil, brown sugar, lemongrass, and fish stock in a mixing bowl. Combine thoroughly.

In a large skillet over medium heat, heat the vegetable oil.

Cook the carrot for 2 minutes before adding the zucchini and onion to the skillet. Cook for 5 minutes, stirring frequently.

Cook for 1 minute after adding the mushrooms.

After that, add the squid and cook for 3-5 minutes with the vegetables.

Pour the sauce into the pan and cook for another 3 minutes, stirring constantly.

Before serving, sprinkle with sesame seeds.

If desired, serve warm with rice.

Eomuk Stir-Fried (Fish Cakes)

10 minutes to prepare

Preparation Time: 15 minutes

4 people

Ingredients:

Nepomuk 4 sheets (fish cake) 14 tbsp soy sauce

2 tbsp of rice wine

1 tbsp hoisin sauce

cloves crushed and minced garlic

2 tbsp. sesame seeds

2 tbsp of vegetable oil

12 cups sliced sweet yellow onion 12 cups sliced red bell pepper

1 cup spear tips asparagus 12 teaspoons of salt

1 teaspoon ground black pepper

Serve with cooked rice

Fill a saucepan halfway with water and bring to a boil. Immerse the fish cake for 30 seconds. Allow the fish cakes to drain and cool after removing them from the water.

Combine the soy sauce, rice wine, hoisin sauce, garlic, and sesame seeds in a mixing bowl. Combine thoroughly.

In a large skillet or wok, heat the vegetable oil over medium-high heat.

Cook for 3-4 minutes, or until the onion, red bell pepper, and asparagus spears are crisp-tender.

Cut each fish cake into four strips. Cook, stirring constantly, for 3-4 minutes after adding the strips to the pan.

Stir in the sauce to coat. Cook for another 3-5 minutes, or until the fish cakes are thoroughly heated.

Serve immediately with cooked rice.

Crab Cakes with Lime and Kimchi

10 minutes to prepare

Time to prepare: 15 minutes plus chill time

4-6 people

1 pound lump crab meat 12 cups diced scallions 14 cups chopped kimchi 14 cups finely diced red bell pepper 1 tablespoon lime zest 12 cups divided panko bread crumbs

1 big egg

12 cups of mayonnaise

12 teaspoon of cayenne pepper powder 12 teaspoons of salt

1 teaspoon ground black pepper

3 tablespoons olive oil

In a mixing bowl, combine the crab meat, scallions, kimchi, red bell pepper, lime zest, and half of the panko bread crumbs.

Combine thoroughly.

In a separate bowl, whisk together the egg, mayonnaise, cayenne pepper, salt, and black pepper. To blend, whisk everything together thoroughly.

Combine the crab meat with the mayonnaise mixture. Combine thoroughly.

Use parchment paper to line a small baking sheet. Make 12-14 portions of the crab mixture and flatten slightly. Refrigerate for up to 1 hour after placing them on the tray.

In a skillet over medium heat, heat the vegetable oil.

Gently press the remaining panko crumbs into the crab cakes' surface.

Cook the cakes in the hot oil until golden brown, about 3-5 minutes per side.

Remove from the pan and set aside to drain any excess oil before serving.

Sun Jun Saeng (Fried Fish)

10 minutes to prepare

Preparation Time: 10 minutes

4 people

1 pound white fish fillets, rinsed and patted dry teaspoons salt 1 teaspoon coarse ground black pepper 14 cup flour teaspoon finely chopped fresh chives 14 teaspoons cayenne powder

2 tbsp. vegetable oil

2 lightly beaten eggs

Season the fish with salt and black pepper before cooking.

Combine the flour, chives, and cayenne powder with the remaining salt and black pepper. Combine thoroughly.

In a large skillet over medium heat, heat the vegetable oil.

Dredge each piece of fish in the flour mixture, coating both sides thoroughly.

Place each piece of coated fish in the pan after dipping it into the beaten egg.

Cook for 3-4 minutes per side, or until golden.

Remove from the pan and set aside to drain any excess oil before serving.

Assortment of Side Dishes

Tofu with Garlic and Sesame

10 minutes to prepare

Preparation Time: 10 minutes

4 people

14 cup soy sauce (optional)

1 tbsp. brown sugar 1 tsp. sesame oil

minced garlic cloves

1 tsp sesame seeds 1 pound extra firm tofu, sliced 3 tbsp vegetable oil

In a mixing bowl, combine the soy sauce, brown sugar, sesame oil, garlic, and sesame seeds.

Place the tofu on a flat surface and gently pat away any excess moisture with a paper towel.

In a large skillet over medium-high heat, heat the vegetable oil.

Cook the tofu in the hot oil until golden brown, about 2-3 minutes per side.

Cook, stirring gently, for 1-2 minutes after adding the sauce to the pan.

Before serving, arrange the tofu slices on a serving plate and drizzle with the sauce.

Salad with Green Onions

Cooking Time: 0

Prep Time allotted: 10 minutes

2-4 people

2 cups green onions, sliced very thinly lengthwise

2 crushed and minced garlic cloves

2 teaspoons finely chopped fresh mint

2 tbsp of soy sauce

1 tsp lime juice

1 tsp white sugar

1 tsp. rice vinegar

In a large mixing bowl, combine the scallions, garlic, and mint. Toss to combine.

Combine the soy sauce, lime juice, sugar, and rice vinegar in a separate bowl. Drizzle over the scallion mixture after thoroughly mixing. To coat, toss everything together.

Serve right away or chill for several hours before serving.

Jorim Gamja (Soy Potatoes)

Time to cook: 20 minutes

Preparation Time: 10 minutes

2-4 people

Ingredients:

2 cups peeled and cubed white potatoes

2 tbsp of vegetable oil 14 cups Korean soy sauce 12 cups vegetable stock
2 tbsp honey 1 tbsp white sugar 1 tsp cloves crushed and minced garlic

12 teaspoons of salt

12 tsp black pepper

2 tsp sesame seeds, toasted

In a large skillet over medium heat, heat the vegetable oil.

Cook, stirring frequently until the potatoes are nicely browned on all sides, approximately 7-10 minutes.

Combine the vegetable stock, Korean soy sauce, honey, sugar, garlic, salt, and black pepper in a mixing bowl. Pour into the pan after thoroughly mixing.

Cook the potatoes for another 5 minutes, stirring frequently until the sauce thickens.

Push the potatoes to one side of the pan and drain as much sauce as you can.

Return the pan to the heat and cook the potatoes for 3-5 minutes, or until slightly crusted.

Before serving, top with toasted sesame seeds.

Bok Choy with Garlic and Spicy Sesame

10 minutes to prepare

Preparation Time: 10 minutes

4 people

Ingredients: cubes of ice

6 cups trimmed mini bok choy

3 tbsp. vegetable oil 1 tbsp. sesame oil 1 tbsp. soy sauce

two tbsp vegetable stock

1 tsp red chile, minced 1 tbsp brown sugar cloves thinly sliced garlic

1 tablespoon sesame seeds, toasted

Preparation: Fill a bowl halfway with ice cubes. Set aside some time

Boil the bok choy for 1 minute in boiling water. Remove the bok choy from the heat and place it in a bowl of ice cubes to stop the cooking process. Allow to cook and drain thoroughly.

In a large skillet or wok, heat the oils over medium-high heat.

In a mixing bowl, combine the soy sauce, vegetable stock, chili, and brown sugar.

Cook for 1 minute after adding the garlic to the skillet before adding the sauce and cooking for another minute.

Cook the bok choy in the skillet, stirring constantly, until it softens, about 3-5 minutes.

Before serving, toss with toasted sesame seeds.

Jangjolim (Soy Eggs)

30 minutes to prepare

Preparation Time: 10 minutes

6 people

Ingredients: 12 room-temperature eggs

2 c. water

1-quart soy sauce

10 garlic cloves

1 jalapeno or other chile pepper, thinly sliced

1 teaspoon of corn syrup

Place the eggs in a large pot with enough cool water to completely cover them.

Place the pot on the stove, covered. Over medium-high heat, bring the water to a boil. When the water reaches a boil, turn off the heat and leave the eggs in the water for 5-7 minutes.

Remove the eggs from the water with care and run them under cold water to cool them down enough to handle.

After the eggs have cooled completely, carefully remove and discard the shells.

Return the eggs to the pot and add the 2 cups water and soy sauce.

Over medium heat, bring the sauce to a boil. Reduce the heat to low and simmer the eggs for about 20 minutes, gently stirring occasionally to ensure even coloration.

To the liquid, add the garlic cloves, chile pepper, and corn syrup.

Cook for another 5 minutes, stirring gently.

Serve hot or cold.

Korean Radish with a Sweet and Sour Flavour

Cooking Time: 0

Prep Time allotted: 15 minutes

2-4 people

Ingredients: 3 cups shredded Korean radish

14 cup rice vinegar 1 cup carrot, shredded 12 cup cucumber, julienned

three tbsp white sugar 12 teaspoons of salt

1 teaspoon ground black pepper

Combine the Korean radish, carrot, and cucumber in a mixing bowl. Combine thoroughly.

In a separate bowl, whisk together the rice vinegar, sugar, salt, and black pepper until well combined.

Toss the vegetables with the dressing to coat them.

Refrigerate for at least 4 hours before serving.

Sweet Rice Balls in Black and Green

10 minutes to prepare

Preparation Time: 20 minutes

8 people

2 tablespoons of toasted black sesame seeds

2 teaspoons matcha tea powder and 2 tablespoons sugar 12 teaspoon salt 34 cup boiling hot water sweet rice flour

1 pound sweet bean paste

1 scraped vanilla bean

To begin, prepare your toppings. In one bowl, combine the toasted sesame seeds, and in another, combine the matcha tea powder and 1 cup of sugar. Place aside.

Combine the sweet rice flour, 2 tablespoons sugar, and salt in a large mixing bowl. Combine thoroughly.

Pour the hot water into the rice flour mixture slowly, stirring until a dough forms. If necessary, mix with your hands until the dough is firm and smooth.

Roll the dough into golf ball-sized mounds in your hands.

Place a spoonful of sweet bean paste in the center of each piece and press it out into a flat circle.

Seal the dough around the paste with your fingers. Roll in your hands again to smooth any seams.

Bring a pot of water to a boil and immerse the balls in it.

Cook for several minutes, or until the balls rise to the surface and float.

Remove the balls from the hot water and immediately shock them in a bowl of cold water to stop the cooking process.

Remove them from the cold water, set them aside, and allow them to air dry for a few minutes.

Roll half of the balls in the black sesame seeds, coating them evenly on all sides.

Roll the remaining matcha tea and sugar balls in the mixture.

Place on a serving platter to serve or place in the refrigerator until ready to eat.

Ginger Candied

1 hour to cook

Preparation time: 10 minutes plus rest time

10-12 people

Ingredients:

1 pound peeled and thinly sliced fresh ginger root

14 teaspoon salt 4 cups sugar

4 c. water

12 cups fine sugar

In a non-reactive saucepan, place the ginger. Pour in enough water to completely cover the ginger.

Heat the water in the pan over high heat until it begins to gently boil. Reduce the heat to low and leave it to simmer for 10-15 minutes.

Drain the ginger completely and repeat the process described above one more time.

Once the ginger has been drained twice, return it to the saucepan with the sugar, salt, and water. To combine, stir everything together.

Cook, stirring occasionally, over medium-high heat until a candy thermometer reads 225°F.

Turn off the heat and leave the pan to cool for several hours or overnight.

Toss the ginger in the superfine sugar lightly.

Serve chilled or at room temperature.

Candies with Sesame Flavor

15 minutes to prepare

Preparation Time: 15 minutes

24 servings

1 tablespoon toasted sesame seeds

1 cup chopped roasted peanuts 12 cup sugar 14 cups light corn syrup 14 teaspoons of salt

1 tablespoon water

Oil a baking sheet and a rolling pin liberally with vegetable or peanut oil.

In a mixing bowl, combine the sesame seeds and peanuts.

In a saucepan over medium to medium-high heat, combine the sugar, corn syrup, salt, and water.

Cook, stirring constantly, until the sugar melts and a thick syrup forms. When the syrup is done, it should be slightly foamy and bubble slightly.

Stir the syrup with a wooden utensil until strands of syrup hang from the spoon as you lift it out of the syrup.

Before removing from the heat, quickly stir in the sesame seeds and peanuts.

Spread the candy quickly onto the greased cookie sheet and roll it out flat with a rolling pin before it hardens.

Cut the candy into 1-inch serving pieces with a very sharp knife.

Allow cooling before serving.

Shaved Ice from Korea

Cooking Time: 0

Preparation Time: 10 minutes

4-6 people

shaved ice 4 cups

14 cups pure maple syrup

1 tbsp sweet bean paste

12 cups fresh strawberries, 12 cups fresh peaches, 12 cups fresh pineapple, 12 cup kiwi, 12 cups mochi rice cakes cups vanilla ice cream

14 c. rice milk

Rice cereal with fruits or crisp rice cereal (optional)

Directions: Layer a third of the shaved ice in 4-6 serving dishes, depending on the desired portion size.

Drizzle the simple syrup over each portion, then top with the sweet bean paste.

Arrange the strawberries, peaches, pineapple, and kiwi on top of another third of the ice.

Finish with the final layer of ice, then the mochi cakes and vanilla ice cream.

Drizzle a little rice milk over each dessert.

If desired, garnish with colorful and sweet fruity or rice cereal.

Conclusion

We enrich our lives by broadening our horizons and experiencing the pleasures and flavors of other cultures. We live in an amazing, vast world, and by embracing cultural cooking, we are rewarded with exposure to incredible flavors and history. This introduction to Korean cooking was designed to do just that. Preparing food from other cultures can be intimidating for many people. Secret recipes have been passed down from generation to generation, containing the secrets that ensure no dish can ever be perfectly replicated by someone who does not have the knowledge. While this is true to some extent — most of us know someone who has a secret recipe that we just can't seem to master on our own — creating the flavor of Korea in your own home is possible. With this book, you can learn about the history, uniqueness, and joy of Korean cooking.